PUNNY ANIMALS

The Meme-ing of Life: Punny Animals
This edition published by Scholastic Inc., 557 Broadway, New York, NY 10012
by arrangement with Hardie Grant Egmont
Scholastic and associated logos are trademarks and/or registered trademarks of Scholastic Inc.
Distributed by Scholastic Canada Ltd., Markham, Ontario

SCHOLASTIC

www.scholastic.com

ISBN: 978-0-545-86823-5

Design copyright © 2014 Hardie Grant Egmont
Cover design by Penny Black Design

A LOL collection of the funniest animal memes from all over the internet are curated in this little book.

Photo credits
Front cover: Foonia/Shutterstock.com
Back cover (clockwise from top left): ravi/Shutterstock.com, Jim Pintar/iStock/Thinkstock,
Jay Ondreicka/Shutterstock.com, peppi18/iStock/Thinkstock
The following interior photos are from Thinkstock: Pages 4, 6, 7, 10, 12, 14,
18, 22, 26, 28, 30, 36, 39, 41 & 45
The following interior photos are from Shutterstock.com: Pages 5, 8, 9, 11,
13, 15, 16, 17, 19, 20, 21, 23, 24, 25, 27, 29, 31, 32, 33, 34, 35, 37,
38, 40, 42, 43, 44, 46, 47 & 48

Printed in Dongguan City, China by Wai Man Book Binding (China) Ltd

10 9 8 7 6 5 4 3 2 1

PUNNY ANIMALS

THE MEME-ING OF LIFE

📖 SCHOLASTIC

www.scholastic.com

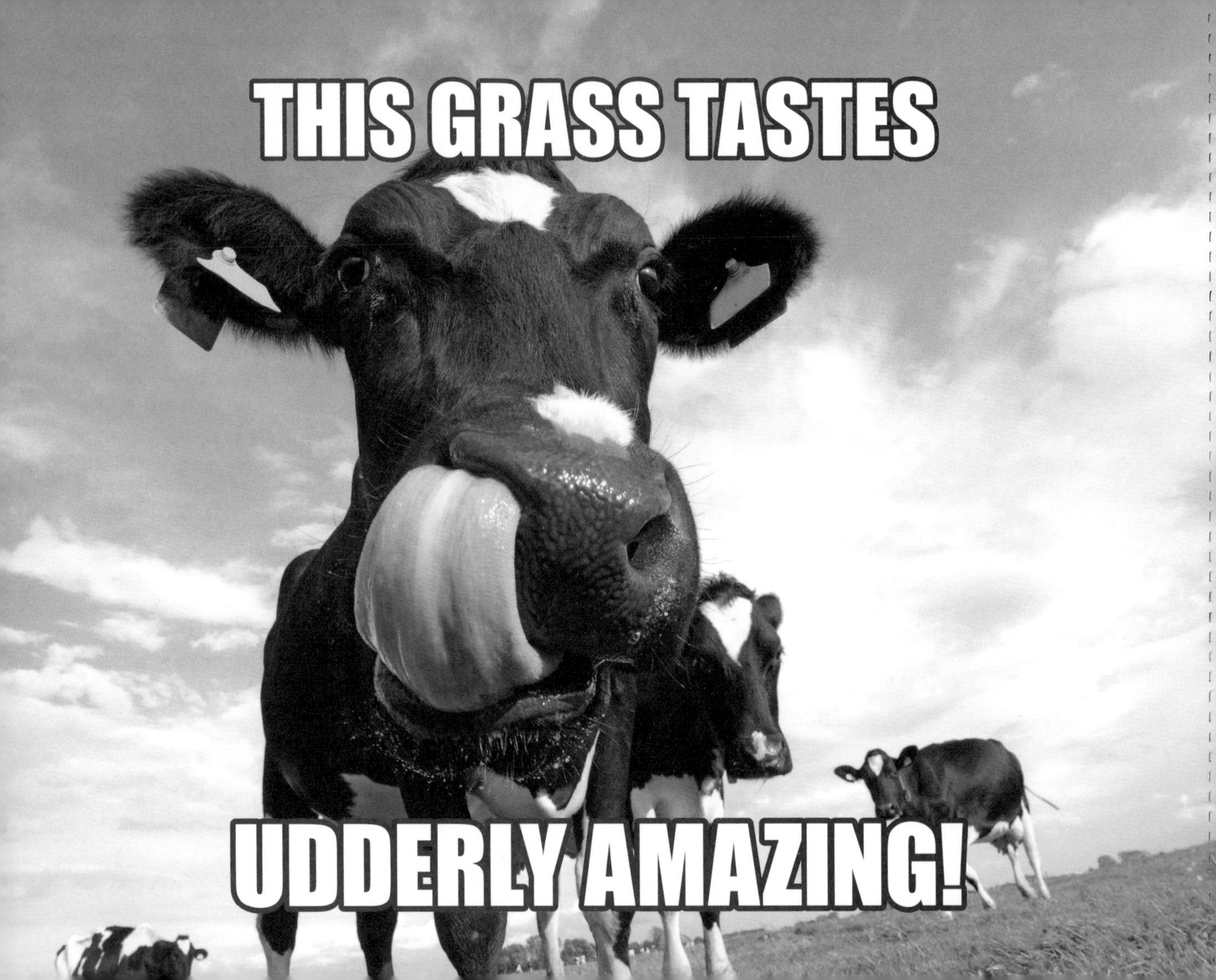
THIS GRASS TASTES
UDDERLY AMAZING!

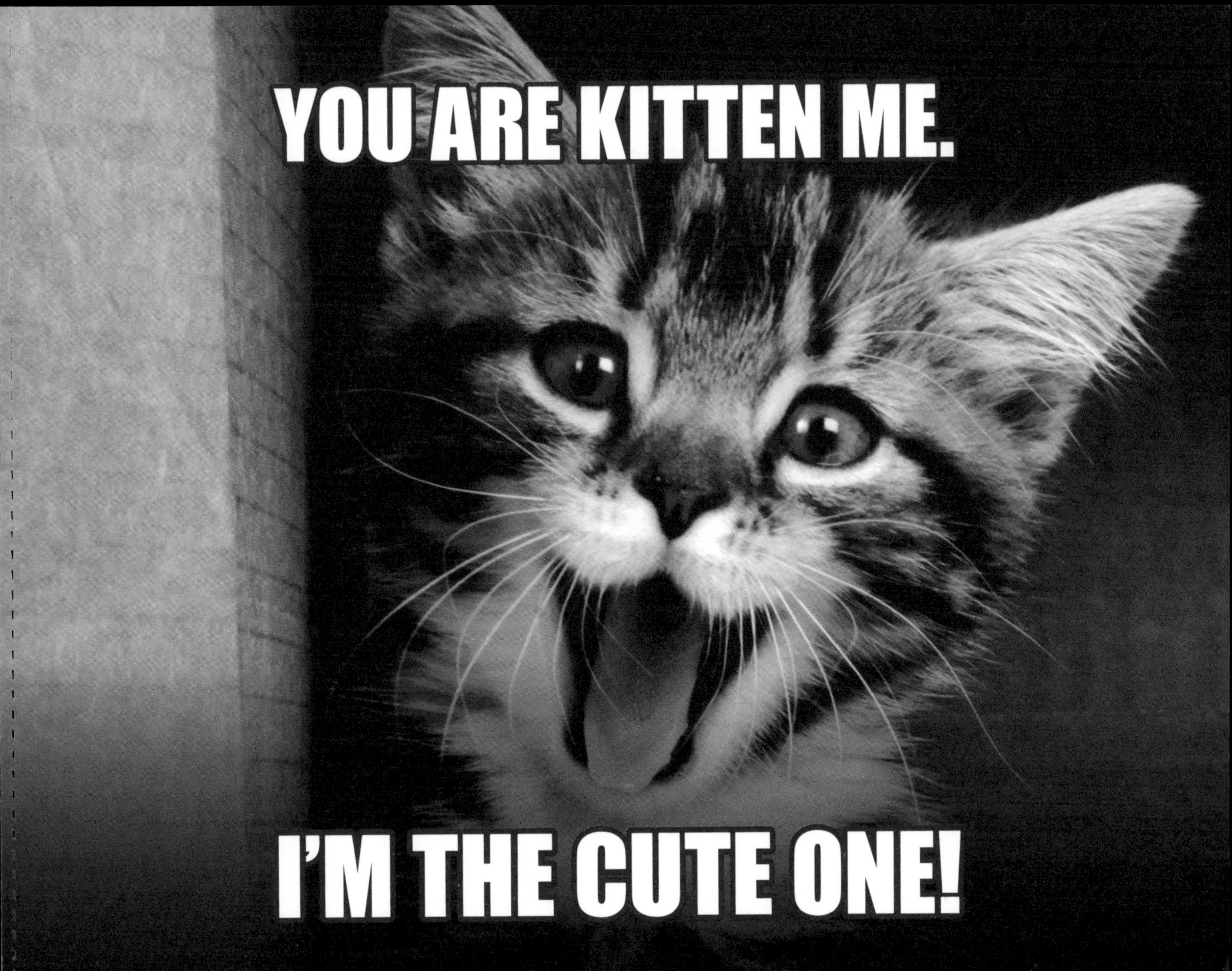
YOU ARE KITTEN ME.
I'M THE CUTE ONE!

I DEER YOU TO

CATCH ME!

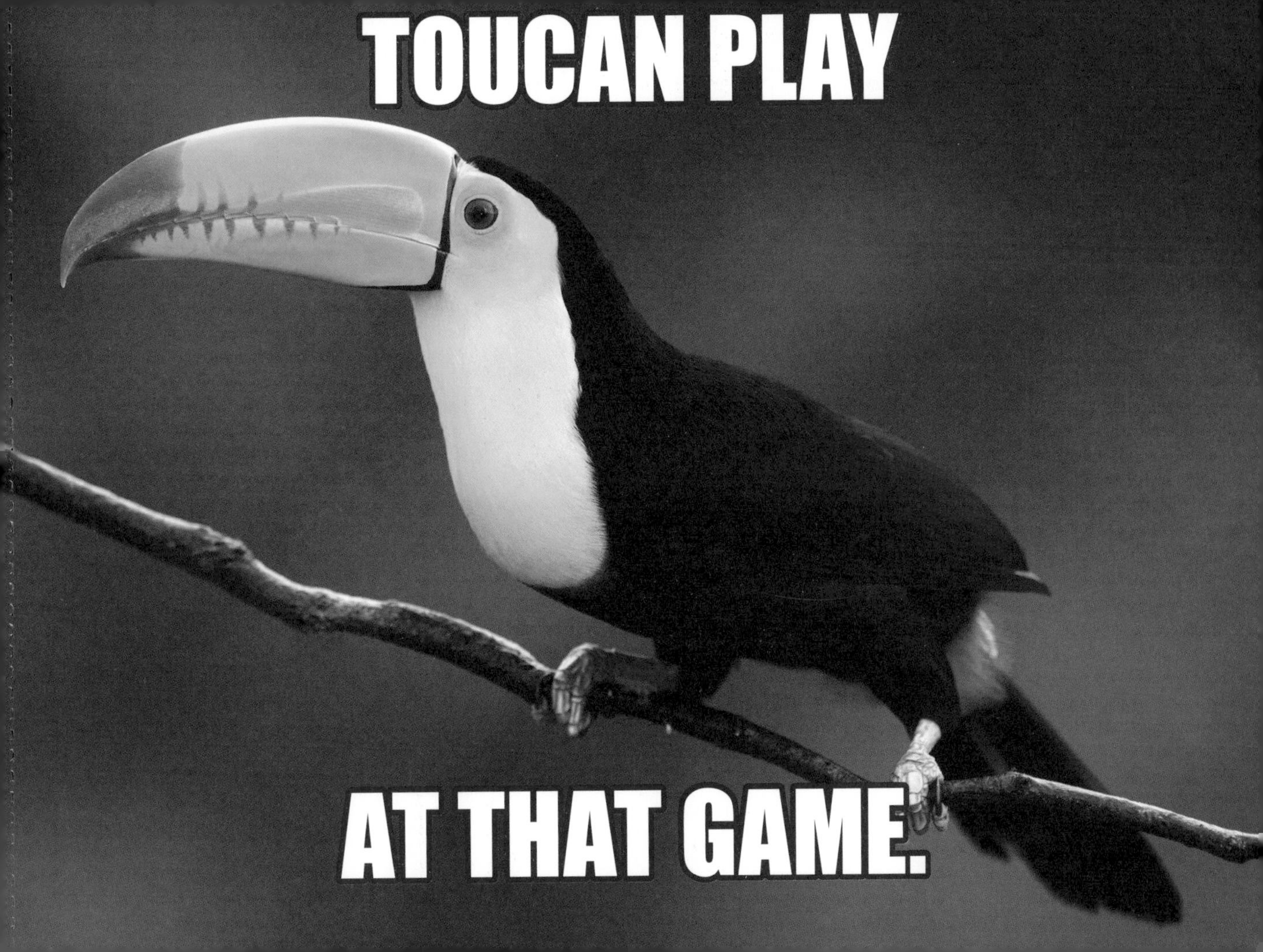
TOUCAN PLAY
AT THAT GAME.

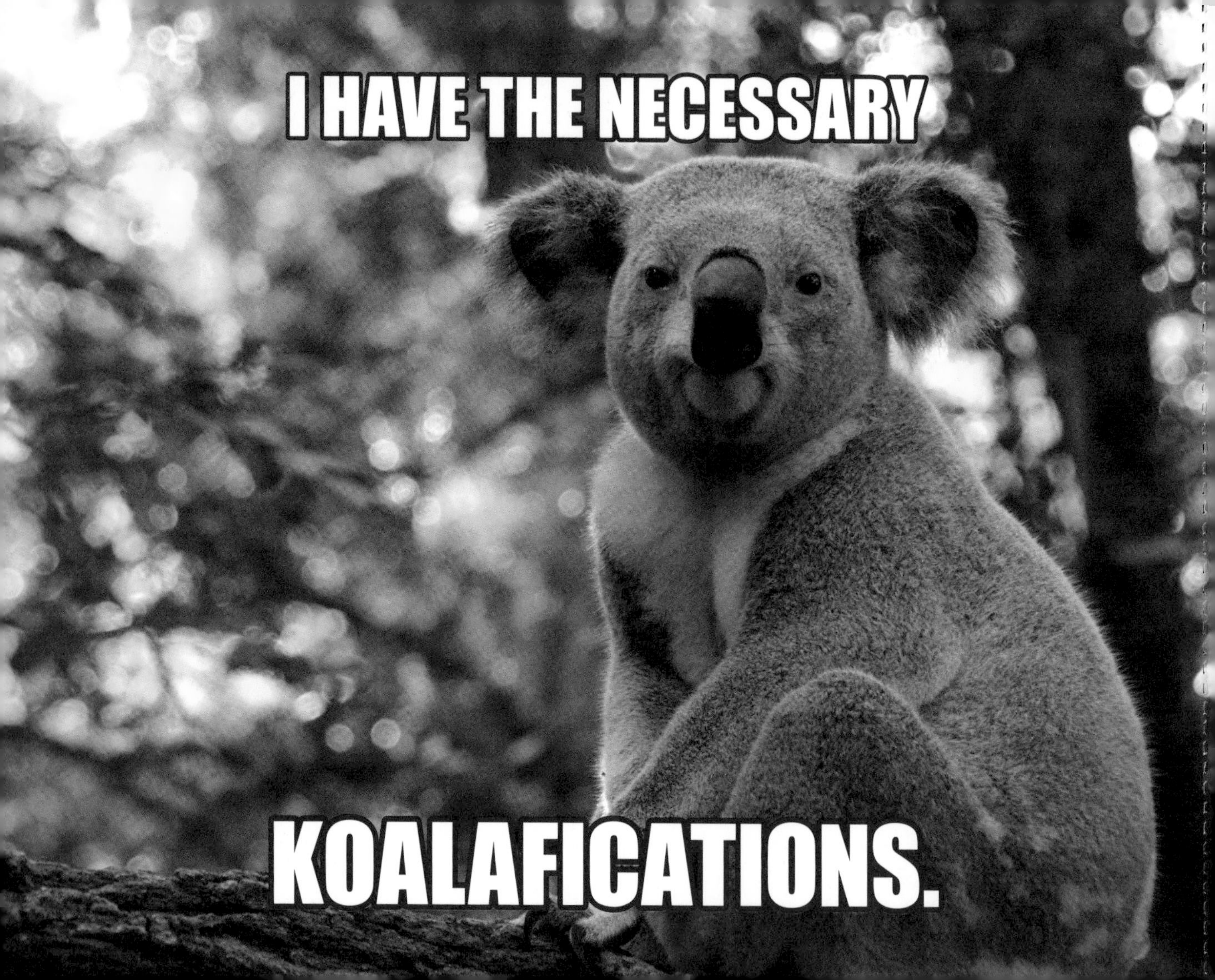
I HAVE THE NECESSARY
KOALAFICATIONS.

I DIDN'T DO IT

ON PORPOISE.

STOP MAKING ME LAUGH

OR I'LL PUMA PANTS.

EARWIGO AGAIN.

THAT SOUNDS
PURRFECT!

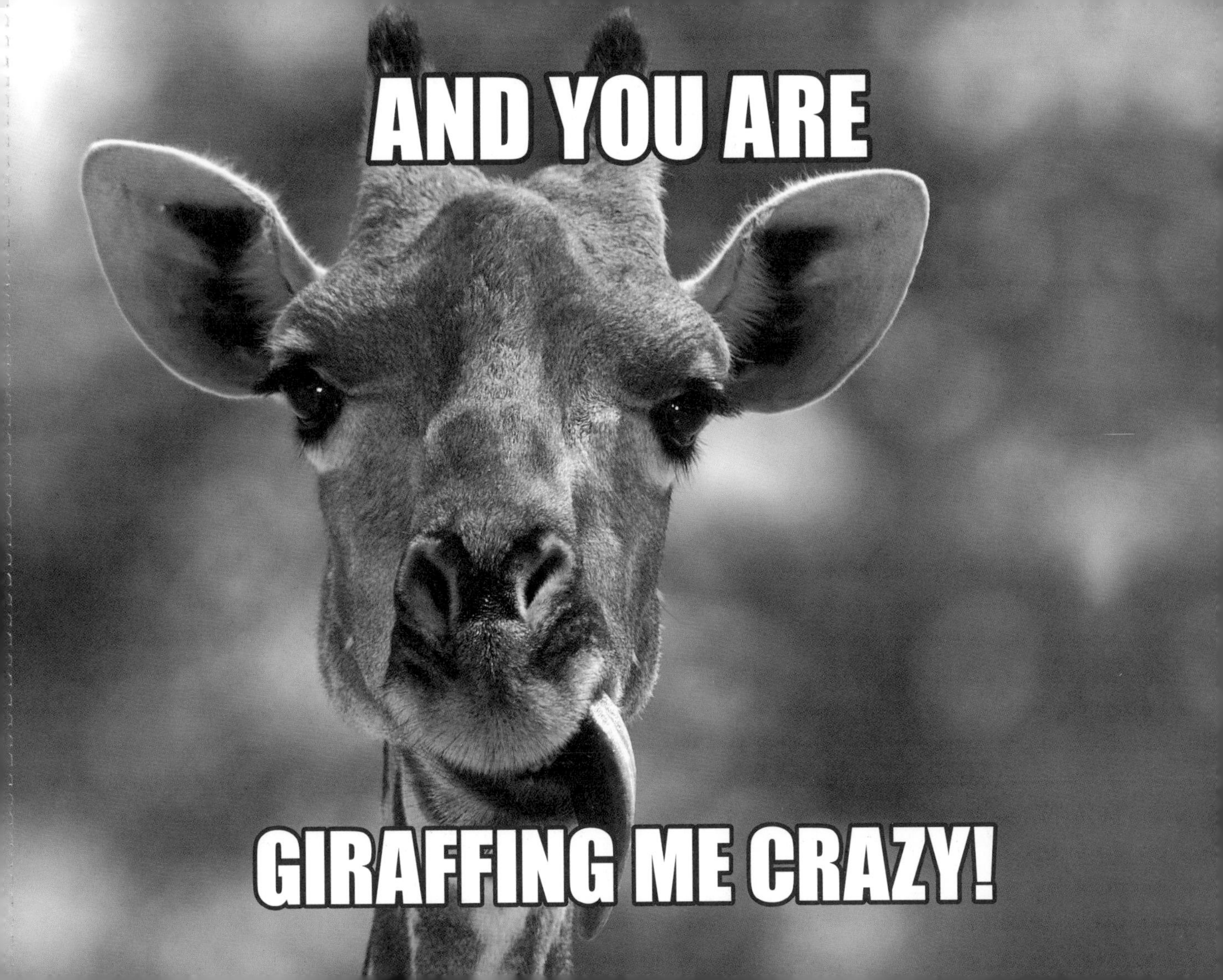
AND YOU ARE
GIRAFFING ME CRAZY!

HOW VERY EMUSING

YOU BOTH ARE!

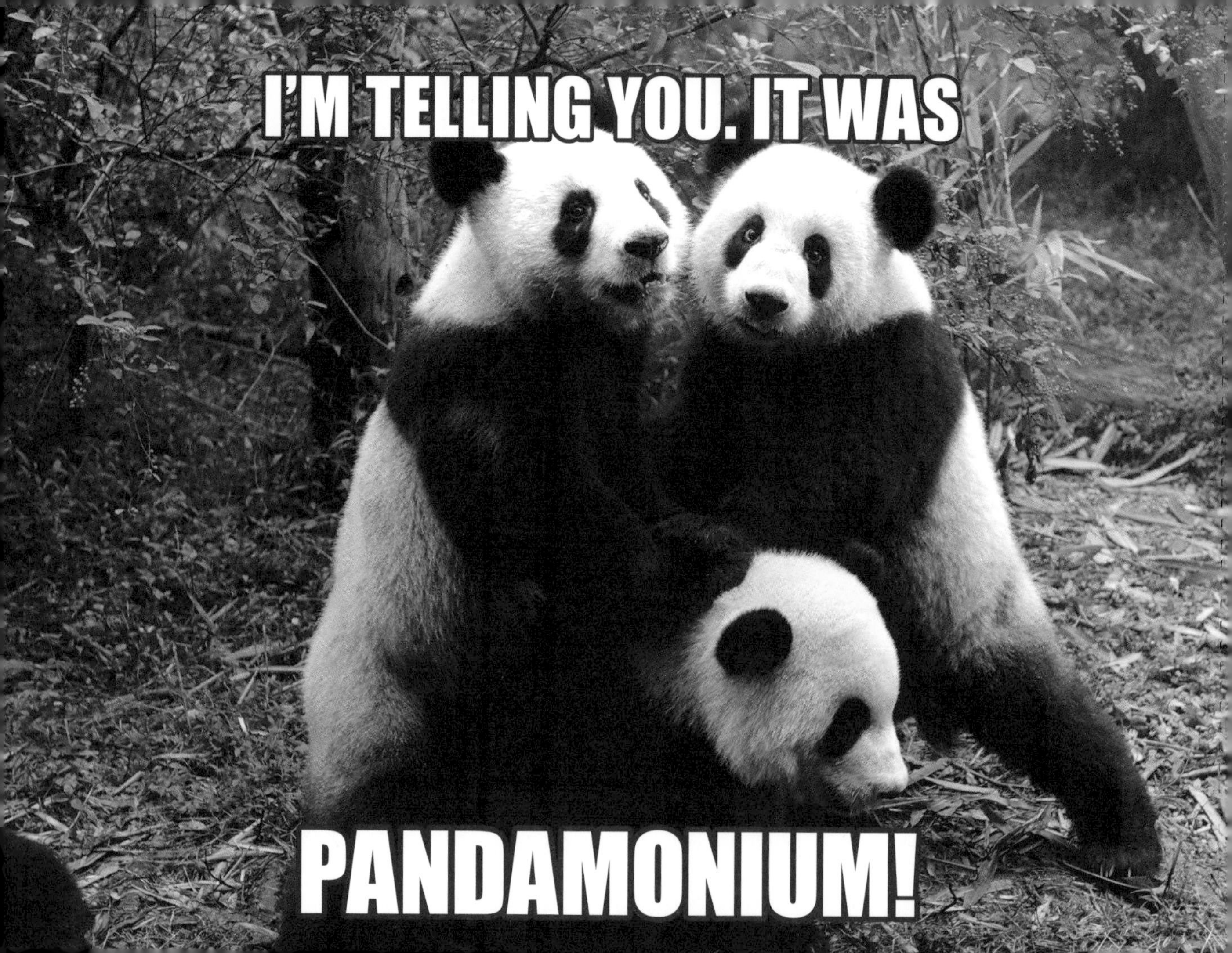
I'M TELLING YOU. IT WAS
PANDAMONIUM!

I HEARD IT WAS A

TOTAL CATASTROPHE.

DON'T LISTEN TO HIM.

HE'S LION.

MY CAR GOT TOAD.

CAN I CATCH A RIDE?

I DON'T KNOW WHY

THEY KICKED MEOWT.

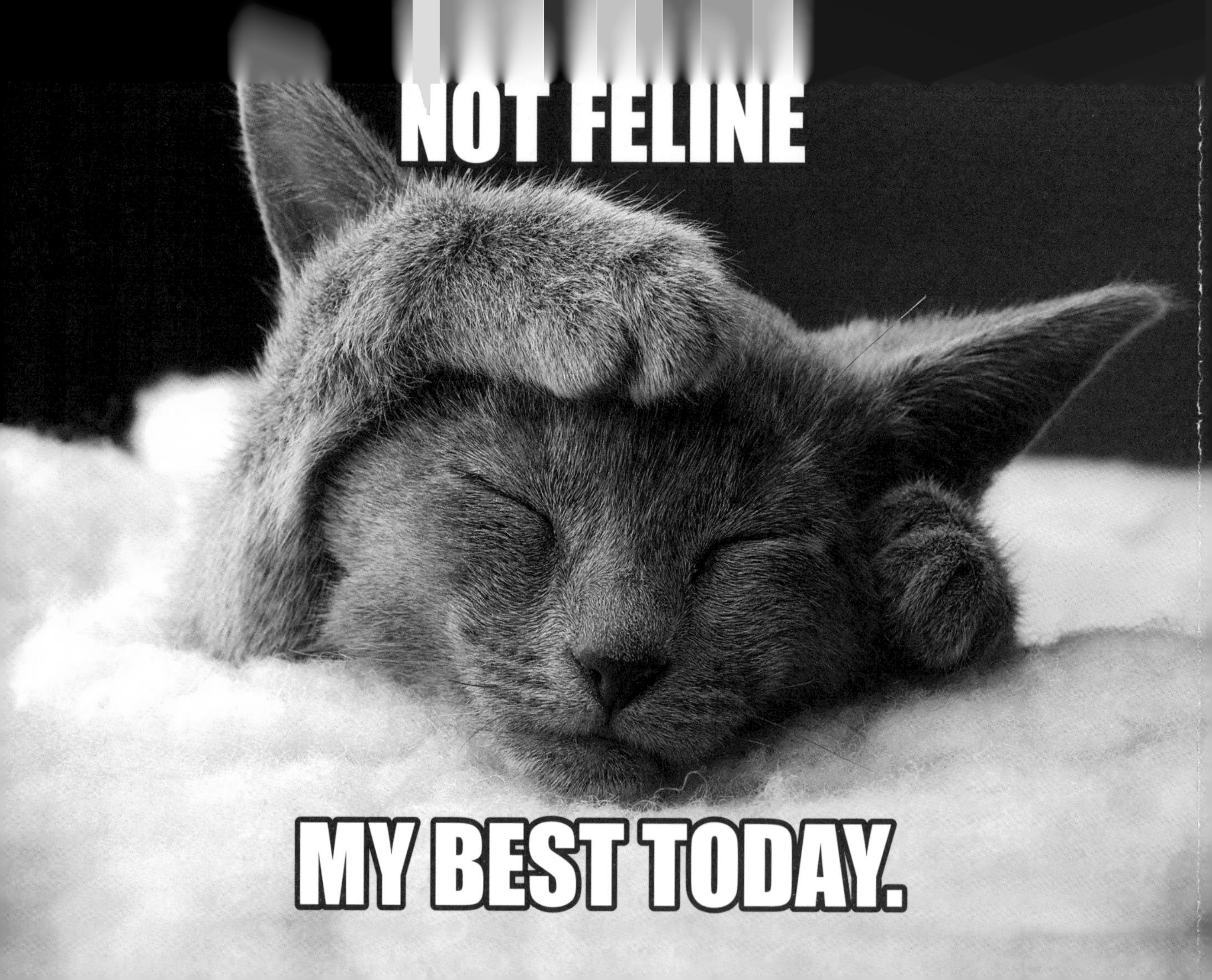
NOT FELINE
MY BEST TODAY.

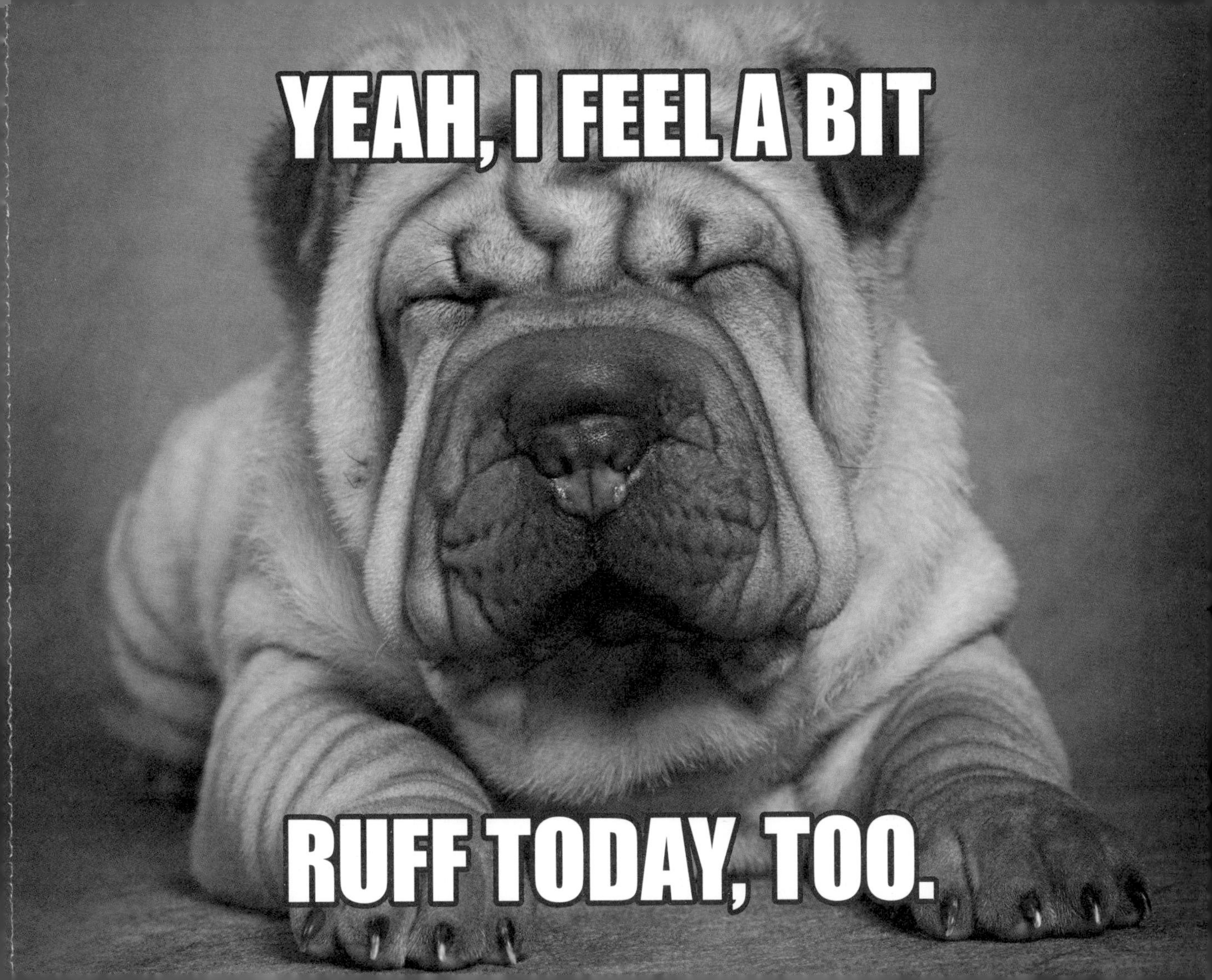
YEAH, I FEEL A BIT
RUFF TODAY, TOO.

THIS ARGUING IS BECOMING

UNBEARABLE.

MY VOICE IS

A LITTLE HORSE.

LET MINNOW

WHEN YOU GET THERE.

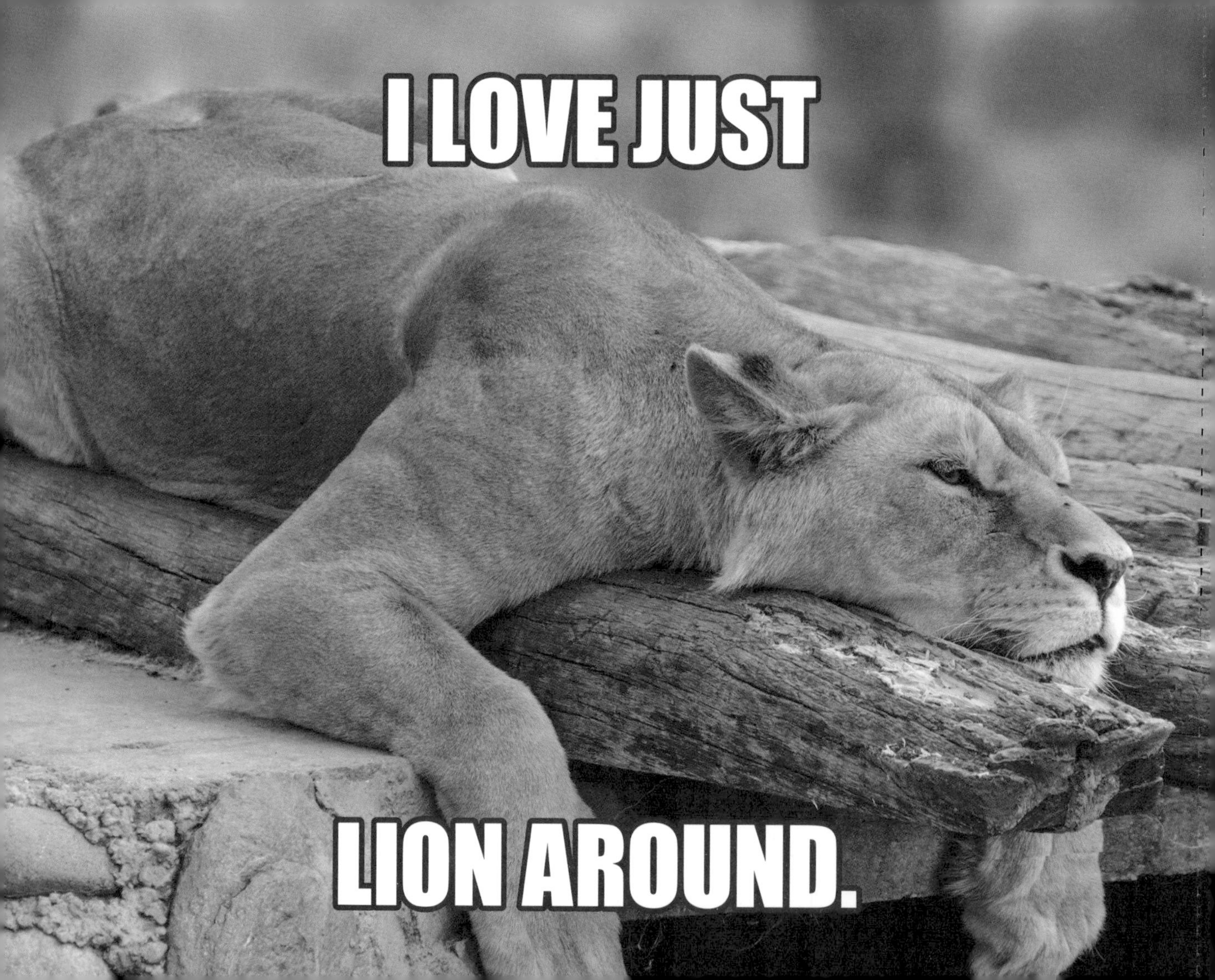
I LOVE JUST
LION AROUND.

GOOD MOVIE BUT IT

WASN'T RIBBITING.

ANIMAL PUNS ARE

SO BOARING.

I THINK THEY'RE

A HOOT!

THAT WAS A TURTLEY

AWESOME BOOK!